To

From

Mums
make the best
friends

Mums
make the best
friends

Abigail Wilentz

Illustrated by Amy Schimler

MQP

Published by MQ Publications Limited

12 The Ivories

6–8 Northampton Street

London, N1 2HY

Tel: +44 (0)20 7359 2244

Fax: +44 (0)20 7359 1616

E-mail: mail@mqpublications.com

North American Office

49 West 24th Street

New York, NY 10010

E-mail: information@mqpublicationsus.com

Web site: www.mqpublications.com

ISBN: 1-84601-047-0

9 8 7 6 5 4 3 2 1

Printed in Italy

CONTENTS

Chapter 1
She was the source of unforgettable memories

8

Chapter 2
Together...

24

Chapter 3
She passed on crucial information

42

Chapter 4
She is irreplaceable

62

SHE WAS THE SOURCE OF UNFORGETTABLE MEMORIES

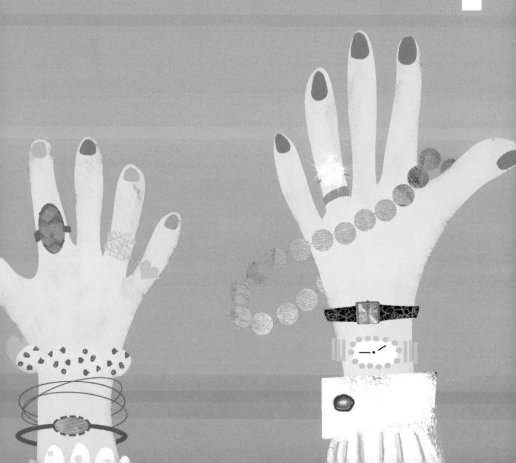

She took you...

...ICE-SKATING
for the very first time.

11

She showed you how to...

...*pet a*

HORSE'S NOSE.

She read aloud to you some
of her favorite books
that became your
favorites too.

She let you try on her jewelry...

16

Sometimes all at once.

17

She helped you choose
the perfect shade of your
first grown-up lipstick.

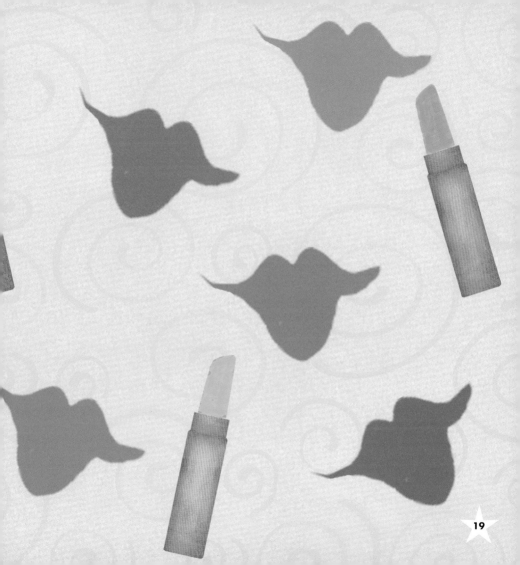

She bought you
your
first

air
of
ttle black **heels.**

21

She urged you to fill your life with rich experiences—fill your passport with as many stamps as possible, taste the exotic flavors of different cuisines, learn the melodic sounds of other languages, and read, read, read to immerse yourself in multiple points of view. Swim with dolphins. Sleep under the stars. Write poetry. Paint. Wear fire-engine red and tango till dawn. You only get one chance, she always said, this is not a dress rehearsal.

Chapter 2

TOGETHER...

You made a **papier mâché piñata** for your **six6h** for your **birthday party...**

...and filled it with candies and silly treats.

You went
"**look**"
out to
at puppies and came
back with a wiggly
surprise in a special
box with holes:

your first dog.

29

You brought home a
SPARKLING
new wok and stir-fried
up a veggie storm.

Carrots, onions,
snow peas, mushrooms.

A dash of
soy sauce.

A sprinkling of ginger.
CHOP CHOP!

You filled the house with

candles

when the power
BLEW OUT...

...then counted the bolts
of lightning through the
bedroom window.

You took long walks
on the beach...

34

...until the soles of your
feet were
silky smooth.

You went to view
the latest museum
exhibitions...

...then debated which paintings, photographs, and sculptures were your favorites over steaming mugs of tea.

You hope
someday to travel
the world...

38

...and get a close-up view of wonderful faraway places.

39

You had your first real heart-to-heart. She told you what it was like growing up when she was your age: what was so different—yet somehow the same— about school, friends, clothes, boys. She described the joys as well as the moments of sadness she had encountered in her life, the major transitions that had changed her forever: getting married, losing her parents, having children of her own. You told her your secret ambitions, as well as your most private fears, and you knew they were as safe as under lock and key.

Chapter 3

SHE PASSED ON CRUCIAL INFORMATION

She showed you how to...

...whip egg whites into soft peaks.

She taught you to find the...

...constellations in the night sky.

She taught you how to...

... curl your hair.

49

She showed you how to swim the backstroke

without making a **splash.**

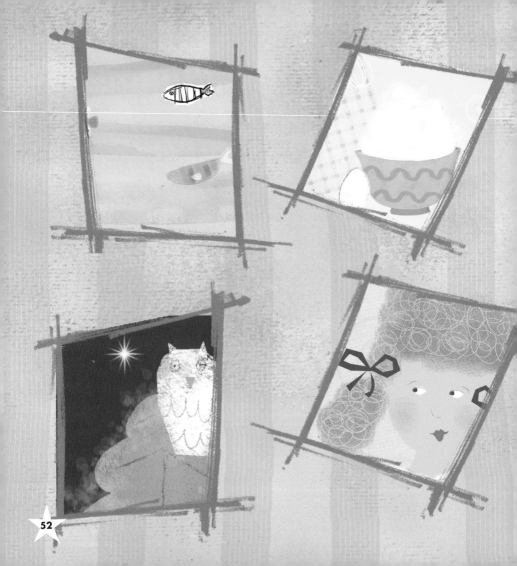

She imparted to you the value of independence. She told you that the deepest self-assurance comes from the ability to stand on your own, from the knowledge that ultimately you can take care of yourself, whatever love and support you receive from those around you. She reminded you that when she was young, women lacked the independence we take for granted today, so you should be sure to celebrate it and do our grandmothers proud.

She taught you the **names** of all the plants in her garden.

55

She demonstrated the coolest

dance moves from her teenage years.

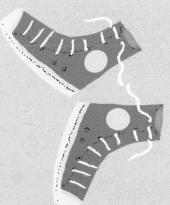

She gave you your first **fashion insights...**

...with a touch of her own *personal flair.*

She advised you not to be jealous of women around you overflowing with dates—in the long run, remember, all you need is one. After all, it's quality, not quantity, right? Finding someone to love is not a competition with your friends and certainly not a race. In the end, discovering a soulmate is a deeply emotional experience that cannot be rushed. Take a deep breath, she said, live your life, and allow it to happen when the time is right and you are truly ready.

SHE IS IRREPLACEABLE

Chapter 4

She stood staunchly
by during that
tHrilLiNg...

...yet terrifying
rite of passage:
Getting yOur
EaRs pierCed.

She let you wear her **favorite**—now vintage—butterfly

nd-**rainbow**-*embroidered* jean jacket to school.

She encouraged you to open your heart to those who treat you with love and respect—that you cannot always keep your guard up against the world and sometimes have to simply give people a chance. At the same time, she was there to bandage the bruises from those unexpected bumps in the road, when your heart was jolted back to reality with a crashing thud, and only her warm reassurance could start you up again and get your wheels turning.

She still buys a **BiG** bag of **POPCOR**

for you to share
at the movies...

...whether you've just eaten a meal or not.

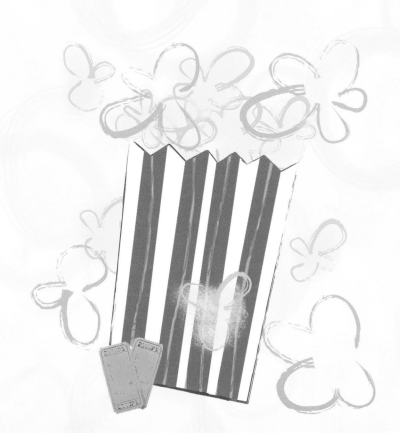

She still listens patiently to your moans and groans...

...when your friends have had enough.

She still makes the **perfect** shopping pal on **rainy days.**

She taught you to expect the most from yourself and believe in your own potential. She insists that if you persevere and never let naysayers discourage you from your goal, you can achieve anything you set your mind to. Who is to say that your fate has already been written? Your future is what you make of it, so dream big, reach for the stars, and see what you catch.

You will always be her
number one fan.